FINANCE KNOWLEDGE WHICH THEY DON'T TEACH IN SCHOOL

UNDERSTAND HOW MONEY IS CREATED AND INVESTMENT OPTIONS AVAILABLE TO YOU

PRADEEP BHASKARAN

Made with ♥ on the Notion Press Platform
www.notionpress.com

Contents

Preface

The book reveals some basic financial knowledge normally which they don't teach in School. It contains basic finance concepts which everyone must understand before investing their hard-earned money. This book is an experiment to teach basic finance knowledge in a very simple English language with related examples to make the reader understand. It talks about the concept of Money, how it is created in the practical world, and the types of Investment options available to people to grow their wealth. Many Engineers and fresh graduates who come out of college with a job don't understand how and where they can invest money in an incremental way even if the income is less. This book is for them.

CHAPTER ONE

How money is created? Gold standard of Money and Fiat currencies

In the olden days, it is believed that people used the Barter system instead of money. The Barter system is nothing but two individuals or parties exchanging items with each other based on the agreed terms. For e.g, an individual can exchange 1kg of rice valued at 10 rupees for 1 kg of vegetables valued at the same 10 rupees.

The Gold Standard of Money was followed internationally in the 19th and 20th centuries (up to 1971). In the past currencies were also backed by Silver. After 1971, Fiat Currencies were used all over the World. Currently the currencies in use today are Fiat Currencies.

So what is the Gold Standard of Money, Fiat currencies, and how money is created?

Gold Standard of Money:

Under Gold Standard, all countries fixed the value of their currencies in terms of a specified amount of gold. Countries will set a fixed price for gold with respect to the local currency and buys and sells gold at that price. In India, around 1900, the price of 1 gram of gold is pegged approximately to 2 rupees. Under the gold standard, a person can go to the bank and give paper money (currency) and get an equal amount of gold from the bank. A country following the gold standard cannot print the extra paper money as they like, there is a limitation. The amount of paper money printed should be equal to the amount of gold reserves held by that government because on-demand, the government should return an equal amount of gold to the paper money. This limitation of printing money prevents **Inflation** (Rise in prices of goods and depreciation of the value of currency). An example of inflation is that in 1990 price of 1 gram of Gold is INR 320, whereas in 2022 the same 1 gram of Gold cost INR 5267. We cannot buy the same asset with the same purchase value of the currency in 1990 & 2022 because of Inflation of the value of currency over the years. The average inflation rate per year in India from 1960 to 2021 calculated was 7.5% per year. Between 1880 and 1914, the period when the United States followed the Gold standard, the average inflation per year was only 0.1%.

How this limitation of printing money under the gold standard prevents inflation?

If there is no limitation in printing money and if the government prints extra money, then households will have more money to spend on goods, but if the quantity of goods produced by manufacturers stays the same, then demand for goods shoots up which will cause firms and companies to increase the prices of goods. So you cannot buy the same quantity of goods (e.g rice) with the same amount (e.g INR 100) after the inflation & price rise. With the same INR 100, you could get more quantity of goods before inflation. This means that the value of the currency is reduced or depreciated. If the government follows the gold standard, it can only print money with respect to the gold reserves held by that government and there is no possibility of printing extra money which prevents inflation.

Fiat currency:

Fiat currencies are the currencies (e.g: Dollar, Rupee, Euro, etc) that is used all over the world today. Fiat currency is a government-issued currency that is not backed by a physical commodity, such as gold or silver. Fiat currency has value because the public agrees with its value and trusts the government which issues them. Fiat money gives central banks (e.g RBI) greater control over the economy because they can control how much money is printed. One danger of fiat money is that governments can print too much of it, resulting in hyperinflation.

Example: Inflation crisis of Zimbabwe in 2008. The Zimbabwe government printed more money to tackle the national debt, institutional corruption, and economic crisis in 2008. But because of printing more money, the inflation rate was 98% per day in Zimbabwe in 2008, which means for e.g the price of 1kg of rice in Zimbabwe which was 50 rupees yesterday will be 100 rupees today and kept on increasing. Prices rose rapidly and consumers were forced to carry bags of money just to purchase basic staples. In April 2009, Zimbabwe stopped printing its currency, and currencies from other countries were used.

Advantages of Using Fiat Currency:

The Primary advantage is that the government can control the economy through its Central Bank. The Central bank (e.g RBI) controls the printing and circulation of currencies thus controlling the money supply and the banking system. During an economic recession, the government can create more jobs by printing more money for employment payments at the expense of high inflation rates. Commodity money such as Gold is a limited resource around the world and we cannot mine the gold metal indefinitely. So the population growth and increase in economic activity demand more supply of money which will outpace the capacity to mine precious metals such as Gold.

How money is created?

Money (Fiat currency) is created by debt or loans. Banks create new money whenever they make loans. The Central bank (e.g Federal Reserve, RBI, etc) prints money and creates new money for the economy by lending the printed money to Commercial banks (e.g SBI, ICICI, HDFC, etc) and commercial banks give loans to individuals or businesses. Commercial banks follow Fractional reserve banking where a part of deposits (e.g 10%) is to be kept as reserves in the bank and the rest of the deposits are to be given as loans to expand the economy. If an individual gets a car loan from a Bank, he buys a car and transfer the money to the car dealer and now new money is added to the economy and the cycle continues. Here the car dealer may buy a utility or deposit the money back into the bank and then the bank use this deposit money to give new loans and the cycle continues. So Money is made out of nothing (thin air) through debt or loans.

CHAPTER TWO

Type of Investment options – I (Stocks, Bonds, SGB, InVit, REIT, Mutual funds, SIP)

Shares:

Shares are units of ownership of a company. If a company has 1000 shares and one person owns 100 shares of that company, then that person would own 10% of the company's ownership. Shares can be bought and sold on Stock exchanges (e.g BSE, NSE) through brokerages (e.g Zerodha). When a company makes profit consistently, there will be more demand in the stock exchanges to buy the shares of that company, thus the value of shares goes up. Investors can buy shares of companies which has the potential to grow and hold them for years and when the value of shares appreciates investors can sell the shares and book profit. Some companies also provide dividends (part of the profit of a company) at the end of the financial year to the shareholders. Not all companies provide dividends. The disadvantage of shares is that if the company doesn't perform well or not making profits, then the demand for that share becomes less thus losing its value which results in a loss to the Investor.

Bonds:

If a company needs 1 crore for its expansion plans, instead of getting a loan from the bank, it can sell bonds worth 1 crore to the public & raise funds. Since the company cannot get 1 crore from a single person, so they divide this 1 crore bond into 1,00,000 bond units, each bond unit costing INR 100. Governments also issue bonds to raise funds for infrastructure projects like roads, schools, etc. Bonds are nothing but a debt or loan. The public can buy the bond and get the interest payment as per the terms and get back the entire investment at a maturity date from the government or corporate issuing them. The Interest rate for bonds will be higher than the Fixed deposit and there are tax-free bonds available in the market. Bonds can be traded, i.e after buying this bond we can sell this bond to some other person before the maturity date. Bonds can be bought from banks, brokerage firms, and bond dealers. An example of an online platform where bonds can be bought is GoldenPi.

Sovereign Gold bonds (SGB):

Sovereign gold bond (SGB) is nothing but buying gold in digital form. SGB is issued by RBI on behalf of the Government of India. For example, if the gold rate per gram is INR 5000 and you have 1 lakh amount to invest in Gold, you will get 20 grams of physical gold. Instead of buying 20 grams of physical gold, you can buy SGB worth 1 lakh. At the end of the maturity period, you will get the market price of 20 grams of gold in return for the SGB you bought. And also you will get 2.5% interest per year for the amount invested in SGB. The usual maturity period of SGB is 8 years and has an exit option after 5 years. So the maturity period is 8 years and if someone needs money immediately then SGB can be traded in stock exchanges i.e after buying this SGB you can sell it anytime on the stock exchange. The benefit of investing in SGB is that the risk and cost of storing physical gold can be avoided and also get an interest payment (2.5%) per year. SGB can be bought via banks, brokers, post offices, and online platforms

Mutual Funds:

A mutual fund is a company that pools money from many investors and invests the money in securities such as stocks, bonds, and short-term debt. The Funds are managed by a Fund manager on behalf of the investors. The Fund manager will decide where to invest the pooled money and in which stocks and bonds. Normally the fund manager invests the pooled money in different stocks and bonds to avoid the risk of losing money. Fund managers charge fees

(1–3%) to manage the investor's fund. Basically, a mutual fund is a low-risk investment because the money is invested in a variety of stocks and bonds instead of a single stock. Investors buy shares in mutual funds. Each share represents an investor's part of ownership in the fund and the income it generates. Examples of mutual funds are the SBI Mutual fund, ICICI mutual fund, HDFC mutual fund, etc.

InVit & REIT:

InVit – Infrastructure Investment trust

If an infrastructure company is going to build a bridge at a cost of 1000 crore, then the company can transfer this asset(bridge) to a trust and the trust can break this capital of 1000 crore into 10 crore units of INR 100 each and offer it to the general public to buy these units. Once the bridge construction is completed that trust will manage the toll collection and let's say it is entitled to get INR 50 toll/ vehicle which passes through that bridge. 90% of the profit from the toll collection will be given as dividends to the InVit unit holders. InVit can provide a regular and steady income for the investor. InVits are also traded on Stock exchanges. InVit project infrastructure can be the Energy sector, Transportation sector, Communication sector, etc.

REIT - Real Estate Investment Trust

REIT is similar to InVit but here the asset is the income-generating real estate such as malls, apartment buildings, cell towers, data centers, hotels, offices, etc.

SIP – Systematic investment plan:

SIP is an investment route offered by Mutual Funds wherein one can invest a fixed amount in a Mutual Fund scheme at regular intervals– say once a month or once a quarter. It can be as low as INR 500 a month. If you want to do an investment you can save part of your salary every month and once it becomes a decent lump sum amount you can purchase some stocks or buy a mutual fund scheme. Let's say you save INR 5000 per month and save it continuously for 1 year, and at the end of 1 year, you invest a total of INR 60,000 in a stock. Here the INR 5000 saved in 1st month does not grow and it will remain that same 5000 at the end of the year. But instead, if you put that INR 5000 every month in a SIP, in that Mutual fund. The advantage here is that in 1st month the stock price is INR 100, and you bought it for INR 5000, and in the 2nd month the stock price is INR 80, then also you bought it for INR 5000 as a SIP. Here the average price of the stock you have bought is INR 90. So you got the stock with a 10 rupee discount. Chances of making a loss are less in this type of systematic investment.

CHAPTER THREE

Type of Investment options – II (Chit fund, Life Insurance, NPS, Gold, Real Estate, and Cryptocurrency)

Chit fund:

A Chit fund is an arrangement where a group of people arrives to contribute defined money at periodic intervals into a pool. Let's say 20 people pay INR 10,000 each a month, then the total monthly pool becomes INR 2 lakhs. Every month there is an opportunity among the 20 members to withdraw that pooled money as per their emergency requirement. Suppose in 1st month 3 people need the money, then there will be an auction and whoever bids the lowest amount, will get the pooled money. Let's say person A has bid 1.8 lakhs and won the bid. The remaining

20,000 of the pooled money will be distributed to 20 people, such that each person gets INR 1000. So the next month everyone needs to pay only INR 9000 each. Similarly every month someone will bid and the remaining people will get the benefit of the dividend amount. Each month people in the group pay lesser than the required INR 10,000 month for the next 20 months and at the end of maturity, they get the lump sum amount of 2 lakhs excluding the organizer fee. The advantage of a Chit fund is that the borrowers get a lump sum amount with a low-interest rate compared to bank loans.

Life insurance:

Life insurance is not only to provide financial benefit in case of death of the individual but it can also act as an investment option to grow the money and provide a lump sum amount at the end of the insurance period. There are two types of Life insurance.

i. Standard Term insurance &
ii. Term insurance with Return of Premium.

Standard Term insurance:

If a policyholder dies during the policy term, the nominee will receive the sum assured in that case. However, if the policyholder outlives the policy term then no sum assured is given to the nominee. e.g: INR 800 per month to be paid for 30 years to get a life cover of 50 lakhs. Here the policy term is 30 years. Let's say person A of age 30 years took this term insurance, if he outlives the next 30 years of the policy term then the policyholder will not get any sum assured.

Term insurance with Return of Premium

In this case, after the policy term the sum assured will be given back to the policyholder, and also get the sum assured in case of sudden death. For example INR 1325 per month to be paid for the next 15 years, and at the end, the sum assured is INR 3,09,000 and the total premium paid will be INR 2,29,055. In case of the sudden death of the policyholder, the nominee will get INR 2,00,000. If the policyholder outlives the policy term, then he gets the sum assured of INR 3,09,000.

NPS – National pension system:

NPS is an Indian government-sponsored pension scheme, where the individual can invest the amount in a pension account at regular intervals during their employment. After retirement, you will get 60% of the corpus in return as a lump sum amount and the remaining 40% of the corpus will be kept at the pension fund and received as a monthly pension. In NPS scheme minimum contribution of INR 6000 per year can be made as a one-time payment or a monthly installment of INR 500. NPS will give a return of 9-12% interest. A portion of the NPS fund will be invested in equities (stocks) for a better return. NPS holders can claim a tax benefit of a maximum of 1.5 lakhs under section 80C of Income tax.

Gold:

Gold was used as money from 600 BCE and the gold standard of the monetary system was followed throughout the world from 1870 to 1971, where a fixed value of a currency is pegged to Gold. Gold is respected throughout the world for its value and rich history. Investing in gold reduces the risk of inflation as gold retains its value whereas the buying power of currencies loses its value over time. In 2015 Gold price (per 10 grams) is INR 26,343, whereas in 2020 the Gold price (per 10 grams) is INR 48,651. Gold is considered to be the safest investment compared to other investment options.

Real estate:

Real estate is nothing but land or building someone owns. Investment in land results in appreciation (increase in price) of land value over the years. For example, In Chennai, the rates of residential land prices grew at an annual rate of 18% year on year between 2018t to 2021. Investment in a housing property or building provides a regular rental income, property value appreciation (increase in price), and tax benefits. RBI data shows that property rates increased by an average of 15.1% year on year across the major cities in India between 2011 and 2021. Real estate investment is an effective tool against currency depreciation (losing value) due to inflation.

Cryptocurrency:

Cryptocurrency is a digital currency that can be used as a mode of digital payment, which is not controlled by any Government or Bank. It is a decentralized system where each transaction is recorded in a public ledger. The government of India does not recognize cryptocurrencies as legal Currency but approves to use them in utility projects, trading (with huge tax,) and the laws may change in the future. Examples of cryptocurrencies are Bitcoin, Ether, Matic, etc. Some crypto systems have their own use case and utility. For e.g Ethereum is a decentralized blockchain system that uses Ether as a Cryptocurrency. Ethereum is a platform where developers can develop decentralized apps and NFT. Crypto currencies are considered to be high-risk investments because of high volatility in prices and often some cryptocurrencies are de-listed from the exchange platform because of instability or fraud. Cryptocurrencies can be bought and sold in Cryptocurrency exchanges such as Wazirx, CoinDcx etc.

CHAPTER FOUR

Concept of Stocks/ Shares/Equity - IPO, Index funds

Stocks are also called Shares or Equity. In 1600, Dutch and British shipowners travel to the eastern countries via sea to transport goods back to Europe and made a profit. The travel by sea was itself very risky because of pirates and the common risk of weather and poor navigation. To lessen the risk, the ship owners would seek investors to put up money for their sea travel and ships in return for a percentage of the profits if the travel is successful. East India Company issued Shares on paper to investors when they receive money and returns the profit for their shares after the travel. The Dutch East India Company founded in 1602 is the first company to give dividends to the investors for all their profits made through sea travels. The investors also sold this share paper to other investors for profit. More people participated and demand grew for shares. In those times if an investor want to buy shares he would have to track down a broker to carry out a trade. Most transactions happened in Coffee shops and shares for sale were written up on the shop's door. The first Stock exchange in London was officially formed in 1773. The stock exchange is a platform where investors can buy and sell Shares through a broker.

Owning Shares means that the shareholder owns a part of the company equal to the proportionate quantity of shares held by that shareholder. Let's say an Individual owns 100 shares of a company with 1000 outstanding shares. The company's total number of shares is 1000 and the individual holds 10% shares of that company, which means that the Individual owns 10% ownership of that company.

IPO – Initial Public offering

When a company wants to raise money from public investors for its expansion, then the company approaches Stock exchanges to list its company and issue its shares to public. This first-time listing of a company on a Stock exchange by issuing shares to raise money is called Initial Public Offering (IPO). Once the company is listed on a Stock exchange, the shares of that company will be traded (buying & selling) in the exchange. Before IPO the Company is called Private and after the IPO it is called a publicly listed company. Example: Nykaa Company applied for IPO in October 2021 in the stock exchanges (BSE & NSE) in India. Total issue size: 2.64 crore shares, Offered price range of a Share: INR 1085 to INR 1125. Nykaa IPO received bids of over 216.59 crore shares against 2.64 crores, which means it subscribed 81.78 times. Because of the oversubscription, Nykaa's shares were listed at INR 2000 on the stock exchanges. There are IPO of companies where there is no demand for that company's share in IPO which leads to less subscription and leads to lesser price than the offered price range in IPO.

Index funds:

BSE (Bombay stock exchange) and NSE (National stock exchange) are the two stock exchanges in India. The first organized stock exchange (BSE) was started in 1875 in Bombay. In 1986, the BSE index was formed which is called **Sensex.** The words 'Sensitivity' and 'Index' forms Sensex. Sensex was adopted for gauging the performance of the Indian markets. Sensex represents whether the market is performing well (Sensex goes up) or badly (Sensex goes down). This index 'Sensex' consist of 30 stocks that are the country's financially sound and largest companies listed on the BSE. Sensex value is calculated based on a Free-Float capitalization method which uses the market capitalization of all 30 companies with different weightages based on the industry sector of the companies. So when most of the shares of these 30 companies come down then the value of Sensex comes down and vice versa. Market capitalization also referred to as Market cap, is one of the ways of calculating the value of the company. If a Company's total number of Shares is 10,000 and the current share price is INR 100, then the market cap of the company is calculated by multiplying the Total number of shares by the current share price which is 10 lakhs. Apart from BSE Sensex, there are other indexes in BSE such as BSE small cap, BSE Midcap, BSE Large cap, BSE 500 etc. 30 companies in Sensex will change based on their performance. The Sensex value in October'2022 is 59,959.

NSE established in 1992 was the first exchange in the country to provide a modern, fully automated screen-based electronic trading system. Nifty 50 is the benchmark index of the NSE similar to the Sensex. Nifty 50 evaluates the performance of the top 50 best-performing stocks on the NSE. Apart from Nifty 50 there are other indexes in NSE such as Nifty Next 50, Nifty 500, etc. 50 Companies in Nifty50 also will change based on their performance. Nifty 50 value in October'2022 is 17,786.

Index funds are similar to Mutual funds, but here in Index funds the manager will copy the exact number of companies in the index and invest in them. If any two companies go out of the index then two new companies come in, then the index fund will take out the investment of ousted companies and invest in only the current companies in the index. So the performance of the index fund will be directly based on the performance of the Index.

CHAPTER FIVE

Which option is better to build wealth? Investment in Stocks or Trading in Stock?

Investment in stocks:

Stock investing has long been recognized as a powerful technique for accumulating wealth. Investing in Stocks means buying stocks of a Company that has the potential to grow and hold it for long a time(2 years or more) so the stock price will appreciate(increase in price) over time and then stocks can be sold in exchange and make a profit. Here the key point is "holding the stocks for a long time". Normally when the company makes profits the demand for that stocks increases and more people want to buy the stocks of that company, since the demand is more the stock price will increase. So when the company makes a consistent profit over a long time the stock price keeps increasing. When the company doesn't make profits the demand for that stock will be less and hence the stock price comes down. The important consideration is to select fundamentally strong companies which have the potential to grow in the future.

For example, i) Stock price of Bajaj Finance limited on 26th October 2018 is INR 2338 and after four years on 28th October 2022, the stock price is INR 7004. In the period of 4 years, the stock price of Bajaj Finance limited appreciated by 250% which is a huge return.

ii) Stock price of Suzlon energy limited on 4th January 2008 is INR 373 and after four years the stock price on 13th Jan 2012 is INR 20. In 4 years thc stock price of Suzlon energy was reduced by 94%, which is a huge loss to the investor. So the important thing is to monitor the company's performance quarterly and monitor the news about the company. If there is any management or fraud in the company or any new regulations by the government which affects the sector in which the company operates and its profits, then better to sell the stocks and invest in good companies. A website to monitor the news about the performance of the company is https://www.screener.in/, which gives you a mail alcrt about the company. Some companies provide dividends (part of the earnings of the company) for the shareholders, so it will be an additional income for the investors.

Trading in Stocks:

Trading in stocks is nothing but buying the shares and when the share price increases, selling the shares in a very short term on a daily basis or weeks. The problem lies in the fact that after buying the shares if the share price decreases then the trader sell the shares immediately to reduce the loss further in the assumption that the share price will decrease further. When the trader does this activity (buying & selling of shares) many times there is a possibility of huge losses than gains in a few trades. Short-term price changes in shares depend on many factors such as weak quarterly performance of the company, Market sentiment, RBI monetary policy, Government policies, Economic well-being of a country, Geopolitical issues, etc.

CHAPTER SIX

Is Bitcoin an alternative to money? What are bitcoin and Cryptocurrencies?

Bitcoin and Cryptocurrencies:

Bitcoin is a type of Cryptocurrency. Bitcoin is a digital currency designed to act as money and a form of payment outside the control of the Bank. Let's say that person A is in India and B is in the USA, if A wants to send money to B then A cannot directly send money to B. A has to send the money to Bank and the Bank converts the rupee into the dollar and charges a fee and then sends money to B in the USA. But A can send Bitcoin directly to B without any intermediary such as Bank. Bitcoin was developed by Satoshi Nakamoto in 2009. Bitcoin is a decentralized digital currency that operates through the blockchain system. Decentralized means there is no central control like a Bank. But how Bitcoin can be safely transferred without any fraud, here blockchain technology plays a bigger role.

A blockchain is a distributed database or ledger that is shared among the people's computer systems (also called nodes) of a computer network. Let's examine blockchain technology with the transactions of a Bitcoin. When A transfer a bitcoin to B, there has to be someone who verifies it. There are thousands of people located around the globe who wants to verify the transactions. They are called Miners. When A transfers bitcoins to B these transaction details are sent to all Miners across the globe and once all of them verifies, a block is created. The created block has the transaction details and a unique cryptic code (Hash) is created along with the formation of the block. So every time a transaction happens a block is formed which stores the transaction details, a hash code, and also the previous block's hash code. If anyone changes any transaction details in a block then the hash value will be changed for that block, now there is a mismatch between the hash value stored in the changed block and the next block which is easy to detect and identify the fraud. If there is any tampering with any one block, then there will be a mismatch of data among the miners, so miners will reject the transaction. This way when all the transaction data is shared among multiple people then the chances of fraud are nearly impossible. Apart from powering bitcoin, Blockchain technology has uses in many applications such as real-time tracking of goods in the supply chain, healthcare, real estate, Media, etc. Bitcoin can be bought and sold in Cryptocurrency exchanges and converted into cash through the exchanges.

The total bitcoin supply is 21 million. Bitcoin prices are very volatile, In Dec 2017 bitcoin price was USD 19,000 per bitcoin, and in March 2020 bitcoin price was USD 4000 per bitcoin. Bitcoin can be bought in fractions also. We can store bitcoins in Crypto exchanges, they can also be stored in hardware wallets such as pen drives.

Altcoins means Alternate coins. Altcoins are also Cryptocurrencies that are not Bitcoins. Examples of Altcoins are Ether, Litecoins, Matic, etc. Why these altcoins exist, is because of their specific use cases. Let's discuss use cases of Altcoins such as Litecoin and Ether

Litecoin:

For a bitcoin transaction to take place it takes 10 minutes to verify the transaction, to counter this drawback an altcoin called Litecoin was developed. Using Litecoin a transaction can be verified and completed in 2.5 minutes.

Ethereum:

Ethereum is a platform for developers to develop Decentralized apps and NFT. Ether is the cryptocurrency of the Ethereum platform.

There are more than 1000 altcoins that exist and we can buy and sell these altcoins through Cryptocurrency exchanges.

Is Bitcoin an alternative to money?

Ecuador, a country in South America became the first country to approve bitcoin as Legal tender. Legal tender means that bitcoin can be used as legal money in Ecuador to pay debt, buy any goods and services, etc. At the time of writing this book, In India bitcoin is not a legal tender but bitcoin and cryptocurrencies are legal in India to buy

& sell through crypto exchanges. Legal tender in India is the Rupee and RBI released the digital currency of India which is the Digital Rupee. Digital Rupee is a legal tender in digital form. Cryptocurrencies are banned in China and going to release their own digital currency. At the time of writing, Companies like Gucci, Balenciaga, Chipotle, and Shopify accepted crypto as a payment for their products and services. While Gucci will only accept Bitcoin and Ethereum, Shopify accepts 20 different cryptocurrencies.

CHAPTER SEVEN

How do Central Bank (RBI) decisions affect loans, inflation, currency, and stock markets

How Home loans and Car loans are affected by the decisions of the Central bank (RBI)?

The Central bank (RBI) is the only institution in the Country allowed to print and supply money (notes, coins) to commercial banks (SBI, ICICI, HDFC), etc. and it regulates and oversees the activities of Commercial banks. An example of RBI's quarterly monetary policy outcome is "Policy Interest rates (Policy Repo rate or Short term lending rate) hiked by 50 basis points to 5.90 percent". One basis point is equal to 0.01%, so a 50 basis point increase means a 0.5% increase from the earlier policy rate of 5.40%.

Here the policy interest rate is the interest rate at which the Central Bank (RBI) lends money to commercial banks (e.g SBI, ICICI, etc). If the policy interest rate is increased to 50 basis points, then the commercial banks need to pay more interest to the central bank (RBI) for the loans they take from RBI, and in turn, commercial banks charge more interest on the loans they offer to Consumers and Businesses. In such a scenario Home loans will become expensive and the common people need to pay more interest to the banks for their loans. In the reverse scenario if the Central bank reduces the policy repo rate then the commercial bank should reduce the interest rate of the loan which they offer to consumers. For example on a Home loan of INR 50 lakhs for 20 years at 7%, the EMI is INR 38,765 and the total interest is INR 43.03 lakh. If the interest rate increases to 7.4%, the EMI becomes 39,974 and the total interest to be paid becomes INR 45.93 lakhs. So in this case because of an interest rate hike, an extra interest of INR 2.9 lakhs is to be paid for the Home loan. A Home loan can be taken at a fixed interest rate or floating interest rate. Under a fixed interest rate, the interest rate remains constant throughout the tenure of the loan and under a floating interest rate, the interest rate changes as per the policy rate changes made by RBI.

How Central bank (RBI) control price rise and inflation in the Economy?

Inflation is nothing but a rise in the prices of goods and depreciation of the value of the currency. An Example of inflation is that in 1990 price of 1 gram of Gold is INR 320, whereas in 2022 the same 1 gram of Gold cost INR 5267. We cannot buy the same asset with the same purchase value of the currency in 1990 & 2022 because of Inflation of the value of currency over the years. The average inflation rate per year in India from 1960 to 2021 calculated was 7.5% per year. Central banks make the policy decisions to keep the inflation rate under control of 4% in a year. Inflation will be measured and calculated on monthly basis mostly through two indices- CPI(Consumer price index) and WPI (Wholesale price index) – Basically, both indices measure changes in the prices of goods and prices. When the Central bank increases policy interest rates, the interest rate at which the Central Bank(RBI) lends money to the commercial banks(e.g SBI, ICICI, etc) increases, in-turn the loans offered to consumers will become expensive. For example: Let's assume a Car dealer has a fixed inventory of 100 cars. If the cost of buying a car increases because the interest rate offered for car loans increases, then there will be fewer consumers getting loans and buying the cars. In order to sell more cars, the dealer will cut prices to attract buyers. Here the prices were reduced because of the actions of the Central bank to rise the policy interest rate. It's just not one dealer seeing a drop in demand, but the entire economy thus forcing the companies and sellers to reduce the prices of goods and services to attract buyers and thus containing price rise and limiting inflation in the economy. Basically higher interest rate reduces demand and this reduced demand lowers inflation. Prices for goods and services typically go up when demand for them rises. But when it becomes more expensive to borrow, there's less demand for goods and services throughout the economy.

How Central bank (RBI) intervenes in the Foreign exchange market to stabilize the National currency's value?

The Foreign exchange market commonly referred to as Forex is the global marketplace for the exchange of currencies i.e trading one's national currency into another. Forex determines the value of one currency against another in the real world. Forex is an electronic network of banks, brokerages, institutional investors, and individual traders (mostly trading through brokerages or banks).

The value of a nation's currency works on a demand-and-supply basis. For example US dollar and rupee. If there is a high demand for the US dollar the value of the Indian rupee depreciates and vice-versa.

Scenario-I - If India imports more than it exports, then India should buy more dollars from Forex to pay for the imported goods, then the demand for the dollar will be higher than the supply of the dollar and the domestic currency like the Rupee in India will depreciate against the dollar.

Scenario-II - If financial institutional investors (FII) in the US think that India is going to grow and want to invest in Indian stock and bond markets then they will buy more Indian rupees in the Foreign exchange market to invest in India. This demand for Indian rupees will result in the strengthening and appreciation of the Indian rupee and then more US dollars needed to be spent to buy the rupees. Vice versa if the FII lost confidence in making a profit in the Indian market then they will sell Indian shares and bonds which results in more selling of Indian rupees converting to Dollars in Forex which results in the depreciation of the Indian rupee.

Scenario-III - When US Central bank (Federal Reserve) increases the benchmark interest rate, then FII may sell Indian shares and sells Indian rupee and convert them into US dollars and buy US government bonds because the interest earnings from US bond is good.

So In all of the above scenarios the Indian rupee can be sold heavily in Forex and thereby reducing the demand for rupees thus depreciating the value. In order to stabilize the currency value RBI (Central bank of India) may sell more US dollars in their reserves and buy the rupee in the Forex market to equalize the demand and supply of the Indian rupee thus reducing the depreciation of the Indian rupee value.

How do Central bank (RBI) decisions affect Stock market prices?

When the Central bank increases the Policy interest rate, it makes borrowing money from banks expensive for both common people and businesses. This slows down investment and money supply in the market. Now there will be less money available in people's hands to spend so there will be less demand for goods and services overall in the economy. This less demand reduces the revenues of the companies which results in less profitability of companies and so people think that companies will make less profit and tend to sell shares, which brings share prices down. And also companies will cut back on expansion plans because of higher interest rates for loans in banks, as growth plans get postponed the sentiment too goes down and the lucrativeness of investing in the stock market gets impacted.

9 798888 833698

Printed by Libri Plureos GmbH in Hamburg,
Germany